101
Questions
to ask Before
You Get
Engaged

H. NORMAN WRIGHT

HARVEST HOUSE PUBLISHERS
EUGENE, OREGON

Cover by Terry Dugan Design, Minneapolis, Minnesota

Cover images © Photodisc

101 QUESTIONS TO ASK BEFORE YOU GET ENGAGED
Copyright © 2004 by H. Norman Wright
Published by Harvest House Publishers
Eugene, Oregon 97402
www.harvesthousepublishers.com

Library of Congress Cataloging-in-Publication Data
Wright, H. Norman.
    101 questions to ask before you get engaged / H. Norman Wright.
        p. cm.
    Includes bibliographical references.
    ISBN 0-7369-1394-2 (pbk.)
    ISBN 0-7369-3103-8 (eBook)
    1. Marriage—Religious   aspects—Christianity—Miscellanea.   2. Betrothal—Religious aspects—Christianity—Miscellanea.   3. Mate Selection—Religious aspects—Christianity—Miscellanea.   I. Title: One Hundred and one questions to ask before you get engaged. II. Title: One Hundred one questions to ask before you get engaged. III. Title.
    BV4529.2.W75 2004
    646.7'7—dc22   2004001428

Printed in the United States of America

15   16   17 / VP-CF / 24   23   22

Contents

$\mathcal{W}$arning—Never Marry (or Get Engaged to) a Stranger

EARS AGO THERE WAS A VERY POPULAR love song, "Getting to Know You, Getting to Know All About You." Well, that's probably the best advice to follow if you're thinking of engagement.

This is not a book about marriage or how to prepare for getting married. It's more basic than that. It's designed to help you answer the question, "Is this the one I want to even consider as a marriage partner? Is this the person I want to be engaged to as the next step to marrying them?"

During my years of counseling, I've heard so many people say, "The person I married was not the same one I honeymooned with. It's as though they changed overnight. What happened?"

The answer is simple. They married a stranger. There was either courtship deception, or naïveté or not enough questions were asked. Thus, many marriages falter. That's why this book was written—to give you some of the questions you need answers to *now*, not later, in order to make a wise decision.

Let's assume you have sufficient money to purchase a new car. You go to the auto mall where there are 16 dealerships...with cars of all makes, models, colors, vintages, and prices. You pull into the lot, park, and stroll over to this "great looking" car. It's a previously owned model (which means *used*). It's been around the block a few times. But you really like the way it looks and smells, and it's comfortable inside. There are a number of gadgets, including a GPS.

A salesperson comes up and asks if he can help you. You respond with, "You sure can. I want to buy this car."

"Great. What would you like to know about it?"

"Know? What's there to know? I saw it. I like it. I want it—let's draw up the paperwork."

"Well, I can do that. Do you have any questions about its warranty, performance, estimated mileage, or the GPS? And since it's a recent addition, we haven't even put the price on it. Don't you want to know that?"

"Not really. All I know is I want it. And you don't even have to wrap it up for me!"

Would you buy a car in this way? It's doubtful. It's almost ridiculous. If you did, you'd be going into it blind. No—of course you'd ask questions. It's too big of an investment, and you don't want to make a costly mistake.

However, many people who make the decision to become engaged do the very same thing. They don't ask enough questions. They like what they see and that's all that counts. After all, asking questions isn't very romantic...and you may not like the answers.

The fact is, though, at some time you will discover the answers to your questions. Asking them before you say, "I do," can help you make your decision, save you some unneeded heartache, or confirm the direction you're heading. The greater the amount of information you have, the better you'll be able to make a good decision.[1]

I want to help you avoid becoming engaged to a stranger. Yes, it's painful to experience the end of a dating relationship. But, it's even more painful to break off an engagement. Hopefully these questions will help you say, "Yes, I really know this person and feel comfortable in moving ahead," or "I'm glad I asked these questions now so I don't pursue this. It's time to move on."

Better Now Than Later

One of the principal questions I'd like you to consider is, "How is your acquaintanceship?" Yes, acquaintanceship. Jeffrey Larson, in his excellent book *Should We Stay Together?* described it this way:

> I define one's acquaintanceship as a combination of how well you know your partner (depth of knowledge) and how long you've known your partner (breadth of experiences) before marriage. The relationship between acquaintanceship and later marital satisfaction is simple: The longer and better you know someone before marriage, the greater the likelihood of marital satisfaction. This is because the longer you become acquainted with someone before marriage—usually—the better you know them, understand them, and understand your couple strengths and weaknesses.[2]

Most of the following questions and thoughts, however, have come from those who discovered their answers after they were married. They were shocked, dismayed, and felt deceived. Many of the questions are direct and blunt. You may think, "I couldn't ask that!" You may be hesitant, but why? You may think you're going to offend your partner, or you may be thinking *These seem so unromantic*—or you may not want to hear their answer (ignorance is *not* bliss)—or you may be worrying, *What if they ask me the same questions?* Well, your partner *should* ask you the same questions.

You can ask them and discover the answers now, or not ask them and discover the answers later. It's your choice. It's better for you to be in charge of when you find out because, as I said earlier, you will.

In this introduction, you will find suggestions and guidelines from a number of people. As you read them, they may sound like warnings. They are. There's no other way to say it. They are cautionary guidelines. Perhaps that sounds better. These resources are gathered from my many years of relationship counseling.

Don't Ignore the Red Flags

A friend of mine has a particularly powerful statement about his experience with dating. I've shared it at many conferences, and people find it incredibly insightful. I've asked him to share a few highlights. I believe the following can be very helpful to anyone dating.

> In searching for the perfect mate, it has taken a long time for me to discover that there really is no such creature out there. Everything is found in degrees of compromise—*Can I live with this, or can I accept that,* and so on? When I have found one that fits most all of my criteria and parameters, then the question is, *Will I fit hers?* It's extremely difficult trying to find someone where all the gears seem to mesh into place without a lot of grinding.
>
> I think one of the things I find invaluable in dating now is all the experience I have compiled over the years from different situations. I have reached the point now in my 40s where I feel I finally know some of the answers to the questions that I didn't even know to ask in my 20s or 30s. But to this day, I am still adding and updating my list of questions.
>
> If there are any bits of advice I could give anyone who is looking for their ideal mate, it is these: Ask questions of anyone you date and store their answers in your memory bank to see if the answers continue to be consistent with their actions. If something appears to be a red flag, confront it and don't let it slide as "not that big of a deal." Interact with the other person's friends (in group settings), such as on camping trips or skiing trips, or play interaction group-type games. If possible, spend time with the other person's parents (and if any red flags come up, don't ignore

them, because their child is a product of their environment). If there are ways of seeing how the other person will handle pressure situations...put them in it (this way you are able to see how flexible they are or can be, and how they will hold up under pressure). Build a real friendship but stay out of bed, pray together, have similar values and interests in things, come to know the other person's faults and know that you can accept them, watch to see how they treat their pets, and continue to interview them right up to the last moments before marriage....

And as hard as it may seem, if that inner voice tells you that you are making a mistake, at least stop and listen to it. Be willing to pull the plug, or at least put things on hold until issues can be clarified in the relationship—right up to the day of the wedding. It is my feeling that I would much rather be very embarrassed and cause hurt to both of us by putting things on hold—or walking away from the relationship right up to the final days before the wedding—than suck it up, be mad, and live in misery for the rest of my life. Why marry when maybe you know deep down inside that things are not right, or that small things are adding up to be big things but you don't know how to confront them? Why marry just because you're afraid you might hurt the other person by confronting her? A lot of this stuff will come to the surface through premarital counseling. Know ahead of time that some people are able to mask or hide things. If you don't ask specific questions, they may feel, "If you didn't ask, they didn't lie."

As I look back in my dating over the years, I have come to realize how really naïve I was in not even trying to find out what questions I should ask, or in thinking I really didn't have the right to be asking certain questions until I was deeper into the relationship. There were some questions that it didn't even occur to me I should have to ask a "Christian." I assumed she would never have been into something that would be blatantly wrong. *Never assume anything!*

These were words of wisdom that have helped many people.

If You Have to Talk Yourself into It...

On another occasion, my friend said,

> As I reflect back now on six months of dating a very nice woman and think of our first date, I realize now I should have followed my instincts and not had a second date. Even though she was nice, attractive, and liked to do a number of things I enjoy, I still found myself having to talk myself into having another date with her and then another. We reached a very comfortable place in our dating, but there was something missing, I just couldn't put my finger on those missing ingredients until now. They were common sense and a lack of being sensitive to my needs! It took me this long to figure out what I had summed up subconsciously on the first date—without realizing it. Maybe part of me is just slow at coming to these conclusions when the other part of me already knows the outcome. I wanted to give this person the benefit of the doubt, though...And so, six months later I found things no different than in the first couple of hours—except I have now spent six months of my life I can't ever recoup.
>
> I hoped because we had a lot in common, everything would eventually come together with a happy ending. Sure, some things were good, but being able to look back now and see the full picture, those few good things were really like settling for crumbs off a plate when I could and should have been spending the same amount of time looking elsewhere for the full plate. One time I got some great advice that would have saved me a lot of time and energy in this case—*if you have to talk yourself into buying something, you probably won't use it.* So, in carrying this thought into a dating situation, if I have to talk myself into a second or third date, it probably won't work either in the long run. I will continue to search for the one I don't have to talk myself into a second or third date with. (I know there will always be the exception to the rule...but it is nice to at least have a rule to go by).

I am sure I'm not the only one who has found himself trapped in this dilemma, and I hope these thoughts may save someone else some valuable time in their search for the right person.

Real Potential?

Sometimes we find ourselves in a slightly different situation than the one my friend was in. We talk ourselves into an engagement because we see what our partner could become. This won't work because it's a relationship with low potential. Your partner is not what you want him to be or what you had hoped for, yet you find yourself thinking, *But he has such great potential!*

Consider the following such relationships:

- ❀ Perhaps he's not what you're looking for spiritually. But you think, *The Lord could really do wonders with him.*

- ❀ Perhaps his ambition and drive to get ahead is a bit lacking. (That's an understatement.) *But he's just waiting for the right opportunity to come along.*

- ❀ Perhaps your partner has emotional outbursts a bit too often for you. *But I'll be able to help him get a handle on that anger and depression eventually.* It doesn't matter that his friends tell you the mood swings have always been there and are getting more intense as the years go by. (Look out!)

- ❀ Perhaps the way your partner eyes the opposite sex doesn't seem to reflect the depth of your relationship. *But once we're committed, he'll only have eyes for me and no one else.* (Are you serious?)

- ❀ Perhaps the way he handles his finances is a bit scary, especially with all those credit cards maxed out. But you think, *I'm sure he'll learn responsibility once we're married.* In fact, didn't he offer to open a joint checking account and credit card with you so the two of you could learn to more closely work together financially? (That will be a real learning experience for you—like the Road to Bankruptcy 101! Do you really expect marriage to create a miracle?)

❀ Perhaps he doesn't communicate very much or share with you on an emotional level. But you rationalize, *Who would, coming out of that abusive, alcoholic, dysfunctional background?* You've met his parents and they're both cases out of a mental-health textbook. In time, you expect to fill in all those gaps for your partner and he'll become a whole person. (Of course, there may be nothing left of you, either.)

❀ Perhaps the reason he has jumped from relationship to relationship is that no one has ever really cared for him enough, been truly accepting of him, or encouraged him to grow spiritually. *Getting him involved in my church and Bible study should make a difference.*

If you believe in all of these possibilities, then the problem is not the other person. You know who it is...you!

First of all, you can't reshape, remake, and reconstruct another person to this degree. You can't get gold out of a mine that's filled with lead. I've seen people in marriages like this. They end up frustrated, and critical, feeling betrayed and hopelessly trapped. They plead, beg, shout, and threaten their partner, but to no avail.

Why would anyone fool themselves to this degree? Some people feel called to be reformers—they like to reshape others, or at least try to. In doing so, they ease the pain of looking at some of the issues of their own lives.[3]

Every Morning at Breakfast

In the book *There Goes the Bride—Making Up Your Mind, Calling it Off and Moving On,* the following suggestions were made. Please consider them carefully:

❀ "If you have mixed feelings about engagement, don't! You need to be certain. If you get engaged, listen to the feelings, especially numbness or dread or just plain wrongness. These shouldn't be there."

❀ "Engagement is a serious state. Listen to these words: 'Dating is one thing, but signing up for the rest of your life is liable to give anyone a few second thoughts. The challenge is deciding if you're suffering from garden-variety cold feet or what I call, "frozen footsies"—a much rarer malady.'"

❀ "Don't feel pressured into engagement or marriage because your biological clock is ticking faster and faster. As one woman said about making a mistake of becoming engaged, 'I was turning thirty and that expiration date stamped on my forehead was flashing so brightly that it blinded me from all the signs.'"

❀ "If you're thinking of committing your life to someone for the rest of your life, identify the nonnegotiables. Don't do this after the fact. Consider these nonnegotiables:

—If your partner hurts you physically, don't proceed. It won't get better.

—Emotional abuse is more difficult to identify but it can involve lack of respect, controlling, etc.

—Does the other person put you before their parents' wishes or are they controlled by their parents? The scriptural teaching of 'leave their mother and father' includes emotional as well as physical.

—Don't plan on a marriage fixing your current problems. It compounds them. Work on fixing them now, but if you can't repair them...

—If you feel inhibited in what you talk about and can't bring up your needs and concerns now, it won't improve. Try new approaches now.

—If you find yourself saying 'I love him or her, but...' why would you think of proceeding?"

❀ Remember, a wedding is exciting but it lasts for just one day. Is this the person you want across the breakfast table from you every morning?[4]

Red Lights

There are other red-light warning signs about relationships—warning signs that aren't based on knowing the other person. Some are just obvious common-sense guidelines, but too many people like to think, *I'm an exception.* Exceptions only exist in our minds.

Take a look at the following points. They are indications that marriage is not the best direction for you to take right now:

❀ Are you asking, "Are you *really sure* you love me?" again and again? It's an indication of low self-esteem. Counseling would be better than marriage.

❀ If most of your time is characterized by quarrels and disagreements that never get resolved, marriage will make them worse.

❀ If you plan to live together before marriage, don't. It hurts your chances of a lasting marriage.

❀ If your partner is like a parent you don't get along with, why would you want to marry that person?

❀ If your partner is all for your interests and activities, but then reacts to you spending time on them, this won't get better in marriage.

❀ Don't marry just for sex. Physical intimacy alone won't keep a marriage together. You need the emotional, social, spiritual, intellectual, and recreational intimacy as well.

❀ How do you feel if you spend a day with your partner just hanging out and talking? If it's intolerable, why are you together?

❀ If you haven't recovered from a previous relationship, you're not ready for a new one.

❀ If your partner has an addiction and isn't in a recovery program, you're not their therapist. And promises to reform aren't a basis for marriage.

❀ If the two of you are totally opposite, what delights you now will probably be a pain in the neck later.[5]

There are many more. If you need them, check out *Should We Stay Together?* by Jeffrey Larson. I would also suggest *Relationships That Work (And Those That Don't)*, which I've written to help couples make better decisions. Actually, the questions in the remainder of this book will give you more guidelines.

Maybe after reading this information, you're even more convinced that engagement is right for you. Wonderful! Or, you could be questioning your relationship now. Either way, ask these questions before you proceed.

I hope the responses will give you guidance about whether or not you should pursue the relationship. That's their whole purpose. All of them are meant to be asked out loud to your potential mate. Responses can either be verbal or written, and I've left you some space to take notes. I highly recommend that you set aside an ample amount of time to allow for thoughtful discussion. After the questions, I've offered some suggestions on how to deal with the responses. (If you've been married before, please be sure to complete the section in the back of the book, as this may give you insights about your future and your current partner.) This is meant to be a process of "getting to know you," as the song says. Hopefully, you'll enjoy learning more about yourself and your partner.

Two

101 Questions to Ask

1. What makes it easy for you to be open and vulnerable, and what makes it difficult?

The answers to these questions are a road map. First, can your partner be vulnerable? Have you seen signs that they can? You want to respond in a way that makes them feel at ease in your presence and not do anything to put a roadblock in their way. Give them every opportunity. Perhaps this is the first safe relationship they've experienced. If vulnerability and openness can't occur here, how can it occur in marriage?

2. What is your greatest fear or concern about being married? What have you done to address these concerns?

Fears are normal, but are they realistic? Where did they originate? There could be good causes for them or just imagined ones. Has your partner ever talked to someone about these fears to gain insight and put them to rest? If not, encouraging them to do so would be a positive step. It's better for them to identify and face them now than for you to hear on your wedding night, "Oh, by the way..."

3. If you were to marry, in what way would you maintain a healthy "interdependence"? What would you depend upon each other for and what would you take personal responsibility for?

Perhaps you've never considered this part of marriage. "We" doesn't just mean you lose your individuality. There will be both a togetherness and a separateness. You need to discuss who does what for whom and what one does for oneself. Boundaries do exist in marriage. It's like a property line. It distinguishes what is your emotional and personal property line. If someone crosses the line, you feel violated. Boundaries define and protect you. (If this concept is new, you may want to check out *Boundaries in Dating* by Dr. Henry Cloud and Dr. John Townsend.)

4. Describe how you were disciplined as a child. If you have children, how will your discipline be the same and how will it be different than what you experienced?

Are there major differences in discipline styles between you and your partner? Would you be comfortable with their background and what they intend to do? Even though many say, "I'll never discipline my children as I was disciplined," we often revert to the way we were raised. Expect to see some patterns repeated unless definite steps are taken to bring about change. How much involvement have each of you had with children? What books on parenting have you read? Now is not too early to begin.

5. What are five reasons a person would want to spend the rest of their life with you, and three reasons they wouldn't?

This soul-searching and personal question helps you know how well your partner knows himself or herself. Are there reasons you would have for being together or not being together? The responses could elicit some extended discussions. Could you predict their answers? If so, you know your partner quite well. One last thought—if they have no answer to the last part of the question, be cautious.

6. What have you learned from your previous relationships that will make you a better partner for someone at this time?

Every relationship can be a learning experience. For some it makes them wiser, while for others it makes them wary. Note whether the responses are basically blaming the other person. Did your partner learn more about the opposite sex or about themselves in these previous relationships? What would they do differently in your relationship?

7. Describe your spiritual journey over the past ten years, including high and low points.

Perhaps neither of you have ever thought about this or mapped it out. It's time to do so. What caused the low points? What contributed to the high points? Is there a pattern to the journey? Where would you each like to be in the next ten years, and what would you need to do to make it happen?

8. What are three of the most vivid memories you can recall from birth to age 18?

Whether the memories are positive or negative events, who were the significant people involved? How have these memories shaped this person's life? Who we are today is a reflection of our past experiences.

9. We hear a lot today about compatibility. What does this mean to you?

Compatibility means being capable of living together harmoniously, or getting along well together. It means to be in agreement, to combine well. It also means blending together so a relationship enhances, instead of interferes with, each partner's capabilities. A couple needs to work on compatibility in *all* areas of their relationship. Those who become compatible have certain characteristics or skills that help them develop compatibility: They flex, stretch, adapt, and change. There's no other way.

Remember this too: Partial compatibility doesn't work very well. It only leads to holes in the relationship. Becoming compatible is a developmental process, but if someone doesn't know what compatibility is, how can it grow?

10. To what extent do you see the way you both communicate as similar and in what way is it different? What does the phrase "learn to speak your partner's language" mean to you?

Everyone comes to a relationship with their own language style, their own dictionary, and their own patterns of speaking. Some are expanders, and some are condensers. Some are ramblers (they change the subject, don't finish a thought, or go around the barn several times), and some are bottom-line, right-to-the-point communicators. Neither is wrong, just different. People enjoy and relate best to those who are flexible enough to speak their partner's language. A new concept? Think about it.

11. When a person marries, they sever the cord of dependency on and allegiance to their parents. If you marry, which of these will be the most difficult to sever and why?

When a person severs the cord of dependency, it means not being dependent upon parents for material or emotional support. Research shows that those who have completed this prior to marriage have a better chance for their marriage to grow. Severing allegiance means a transfer of priorities from parents to spouse. (By the way, are each of you capable of living 2000 miles away from your parents? It could happen.)

12. Is it easy or difficult for you to pray with a person you're in a relationship with, and for what reason?

Prayer is the foundation for intimacy in a relationship. Praying together builds the other dimensions of intimacy. Author and psychiatrist Dr. Paul Tournier states, "It is only when a husband and wife pray together before God that they find the secret of true harmony, that the difference in their temperaments, their ideas, and their tastes enriches their home instead of endangering it. There will be no further question of one imposing his will on the other, or of the other giving in for the sake of peace. Instead, they will together seek God's will, which alone will ensure that each will be fully able to develop his personality."[6]

Lines open to God are invariably open to one another. A person cannot be genuinely open to God and closed to their mate. Praying together especially reduces the sense of competitiveness in marriage, and at the same time it enhances the sense of completeness.[7]

13. To what degree are you a saver or a spender when it comes to money?

Major issue! If they're a saver, to what degree? Is there a lifelong pattern? What do they expect of the one they marry? If they're a spender, how do they respond to a saver? What about the other way around? Work this one out in advance, or it could lead to disaster.

14. How has your relationship with Jesus Christ changed since this current relationship?

There are several possibilities. Perhaps there has been no change. It has remained the same. Is that because of the relationship, or is it a typical pattern? Or, it could have diminished. Is that because of the relationship, or is your partner struggling spiritually on their own? Hopefully, both of you will grow and encourage one another spiritually.

15. Describe what your life was like before you met your current partner. Describe what *you* were like before you met your current partner.

Changes will occur in each of you in a relationship. Some are healthy, and some unhealthy. Healthy changes involve making adjustments and accommodations. Unhealthy ones actually change the person you are. If your friends and family say, "You're not the person you were before you became involved with _____," you need to find out what they mean.

16. Dreams and aspirations are very important. Have your partner write their response to "If I were to marry I would..." Complete this phrase ten times.

Your partner's response to this phrase is a window into their dreams for the present and the future. It may reveal information you've never heard before—you may be shocked, delighted, surprised, or reassured by what you hear. Being married is meant to enhance and enrich your life, not limit or restrain it in any way.

17. What are the questions about me you've always wanted to ask but never have?

This could become very personal. That's good. You may be surprised. Above all, don't be defensive or offended. Thank your partner for asking. You may want to answer immediately or reflect on the questions for a while. And another thought—why haven't these questions been asked before? Is it because your partner tends to be hesitant or reserved, or because they sense it would not be received well? That's something to think about.

18. What do you think are God's purposes for marriage?

Here are some thoughts on marriage from Scripture:

❊ "So God created man in his own image, in the image of God he created him; male and female he created them" (Genesis 1:27). Marriage is to mirror God's image.

❊ "God blessed them and said to them, 'Be fruitful and increase in number; fill the earth and subdue it. Rule over the fish of the sea and the birds of the air and over every living creature that moves on the ground'" (Genesis 1:28). Marriage is to multiply a godly legacy.

❊ "The LORD God said, 'It is not good for the man to be alone. I will make a helper suitable for him,'" (Genesis 2:18). Marriage is to mutually complete one another.

God chose to reveal a part of who He is and His character through our relationships. Actually, marriage gives us a picture of what God is like. It definitely is a sacred union.

19. What are your beliefs about prenuptial agreements?

Prenuptials usually reflect a lack of trust as well as an incomplete commitment. When you marry, you need to go into marriage with your eyes wide open, but with the intent you *will* be together 'til death do you part.

20. In a relationship, what part of giving of yourself do you struggle with?

Some are gifted at giving of themselves, while for others it's a challenge and chore. Many relationships are out of balance since one does all of the giving and the other takes. This isn't healthy. There needs to be a balance. For some, it's difficult to give of their time or money. Others find it difficult to share personal possessions, friends, or the limelight. Yes, it's a strange question, but one which needs to be explored.

21. What are your beliefs about pornography, and to what degree
    has this ever been a part of your life? How recently?

A pattern of involvement is a problem. Most people today have
run across soft- or hard-core pornography out of curiosity, or
inadvertently because of inaccurate film ratings. The choice to
pursue this will destroy a marriage. If your partner has struggled
with pornography, recommend they seek help now, not promise
to do so "later."

22. If I were a doctor and you were describing your medical history for me, what would it entail? (Accidents, hospitalizations, diseases of any kind including HIV/AIDS, syphilis, herpes, or others.)

Some individuals have been shocked to learn this information *after* they're married. That's when you feel deceived. Some conditions could limit having children or where you live. Everyone's imperfect physically. Learn about it now. Many people marry knowing about their partner's limitations and accept them fully.

23. If something *really* bothered you about me, how would you go about expressing it to me?

The *way* we express our concerns to one another is the issue. Delivery is everything. If you feel attacked, you'll probably be defensive. Some tend to bottle up their feelings and concerns, but these can accumulate, and often there is a blowup later. Proverbs gives us some guidelines:

- ❀ "A man who refuses to admit his mistakes can never be successful. But if he confesses and forsakes them, he gets another chance" (Proverbs 28:13 TLB).

- ❀ "A word fitly spoken *and* in due season is like apples of gold in a setting of silver" (Proverbs 25:11 AMP).

- ❀ "He who guards his mouth and his tongue keeps himself from troubles" (Proverbs 21:23 AMP).

24. What would those in your prior relationships say about you? What did *you* learn from them?

If others were consistent in what they said about your partner, was it positive or negative? If you hear all positives or all negatives, ask about the area not shared with you. Do you see the same traits, tendencies, or qualities in your partner? Hopefully, each relationship was a learning experience for the best rather than one that warped a person's view about the opposite sex.

25. What is there about my life and personality that concerns you at this time?

If you hear, "Oh, nothing concerns me—you're perfect," love really is blind. If you hear, "Well, now that you asked..." and your partner goes on and on, why are they still in the relationship? A few concerns may just be a part of the adjustment process. It's called a growth experience. Talk it through.

If you're constantly hearing complaints and concerns about who you are from your partner, you're involved with a reformer. They could be a perfectionist as well. Either way, engagement or marriage won't be pleasant.

26. How has your relationship with God changed in the past five years? How has your partner's relationship with God changed in the past five years?

Has there been growth? Is the spiritual part of your partner's life on hold? Has it diminished? What have they read? Have they attended any conferences? What is their involvement in church? What questions do they have about God? What is their prayer life like? These are lots of questions but they're very important. Have the two of you read a Christian book together? If not, it's a wonderful journey to begin even now.

Some of my favorite authors are Ken Gire, Max Lucado, and John Ortberg, just for starters. You may also want to read a couple's devotional I've written, such as Starting Out Together *(Regal Books) or* Before You Say "I Do"™ Devotional *(Harvest House).*

27. How would you keep romance alive if you were to marry?

What appears to be romantic to one person might not be to another. Your partner may have several ideas, but they may not light your fire. It's important to discover what type of romance each of you enjoys—that will give you a good road map for keeping the flame alive. And by the way, it won't just happen. There needs to be a commitment to make it happen. And it helps to look your partner in the eye and say "I love you" every day.

28. What are five habits you're glad you have and five you wish you didn't?

Everyone has some habits or patterns. Are yours the same or similar? How do you feel about your partner's? Can you live with them? Accept them? Do they want you to help "get rid of the ones they don't like?" Habits you find annoying now will only be intensified after marriage.

29. Who are the people in your life that have influenced you the most and in what way?

We all have significant people in our lives. Some have been mentors who have helped us grow. Unfortunately, sometimes we are influenced in dysfunctional ways that can hamper relationships. When we identify people and their impact, often *what* we do and *why* we do it takes on a new meaning.

30. Could you describe the people in your life who are the easiest to get along with and those who are the most difficult?

Which list is longer? Is your partner someone who has people skills? If they struggle with others, are the two of you getting along well? If so, what is the difference? Is your partner a person who accepts responsibility for difficulties—or projects blame on others? Does your partner have characteristics similar to the people they have difficulty with?

31. Ten years from now, where would you like to be emotionally? How about spiritually? How about economically? What about family size?

Has your partner thought about their own personal growth? If they're content with the way they are, be cautious. It's easier to answer the last two questions, but the first two are more important for your future. If you're given general answers, ask for specifics.

32. What was your family's economic level and emotional environ-
    ment like when you were growing up? In what way do you see
    this affecting your life today?

Are your economic levels similar? If not, spending habits and
lifestyle expectations could be quite different. How would you
solve this? The emotional environment in your family may have
been positive, but with many it's a mixture. How would this
affect your marriage?

33. When you are sick, how do you want others to respond to you? When a significant person in your life is sick, how do you respond?

Illness is not something you think about before marriage. Everyone has a pattern of response they've developed over the years, as well as a mixture of expectations and needs when they're sick. Many conflicts have occurred because of not discussing this in advance. One or both of you may need to change your way of responding in order to meet the other's needs.

34. What brings you the greatest satisfaction in life, and what do you think it is about you that brings the greatest satisfaction to the Lord?

This is a two-pronged question. For some it's obvious, while with others it's a mystery. Do you have a difficult time with what brings your partner satisfaction? Can you see outward evidence of what they think brings satisfaction to the Lord? Is it a consistent growing pattern or an occasional event? If you receive an "I don't know" or "I can't think of anything," what is that saying to you?

35. What are the "must have" and "must not have" qualities in a person you may want to spend the rest of your life with?

Listen carefully. Can you match this list with who you are and what you have to offer? It's essential to clarify these in advance because these qualities won't change easily and could become demands. Sometimes "shopping lists" are reasonable. Sometimes they're not.

36. What is there in your life that you *never* want to change or that you would never be able to let go of?

This question gives you insight into your partner's values. It's good to know about these now. They could be major or insignificant items. Can you accept them? Would they be a problem? Could you live with them the rest of your life? Where did these values originate? Are your values similar or on opposite ends of the scale? Similar values are one of the essentials for a quality marriage.

37. If you could ask Jesus to change an area of your life, which area would it be, and how would you like it changed? How long has this been a concern?

Were you aware of this or surprised? Has your partner ever considered asking Jesus for help in this area before? This could open up a healthy discussion about the importance of their spiritual life as well as give each of you guidance in praying for one another.

38. What has God taught you in the following situations in your life: failure, pain, waiting, not having enough money, facing disappointment, and facing criticism?

Plan time for this discussion. It's not uncommon for a person not to have sufficient life experience yet for some of these to apply, but in time they will. Others have a life filled with these experiences. If you handle them differently, that's all right.

39. How would you rate your friendships with those of the same sex? 1) "Easy—it's a snap"; 2) "Whatever—I can take them or leave them"; 3) "They're hard work but worthwhile"; 4) "Discouraging—they let you down,"; 5) "Not sure if I've had a deep friendship."

We weren't created to live in isolation. Male or female, we need friends. It's important to like and respect your partner's friends. If not, conflict and taking sides can be a result. If you're "the only true friend they have," you could end up emotionally smothered by your partner. Neither of you can meet all of the other's needs. After marriage, time with friends will also have to be adjusted.

40. What was your last relationship like, and what are three reasons you're confident the relationship is over and you can move forward?

It's important that a person grieve over a broken relationship and be able to say goodbye. They need to be 100 percent certain it is over. If they are still thinking about the individual, it's not a good sign. If they say, "I just know it's over," don't accept that as a substitute for giving the reasons.

41. What do you wish you could say to your mother and father that you've never said to them?

This question is designed to help your partner identify any unfinished business that may exist. (If there's anger or resentment that hasn't been resolved, it could be directed at you if you decide to marry.) Or, it may prompt some previously unexpressed appreciation. If so, why hasn't it been expressed before?

42. Can you think of any loss in your life that you've never fully grieved over?

We all have had losses. If they haven't been grieved for when they occurred, they will come back and intensify the next loss. These losses can interfere with relationships, especially if they are rejections. Do both of you have a healthy pattern of grieving? You'll need this for the future. Be sure to discuss this together. (For additional reading and study, see the book I wrote on this issue: *Recovering from the Losses of Life* [Fleming H. Revell.])

43. What are five adjectives you would select to describe your relationship with your father?

Are these words all negative, all positive, or a mixture? Fathers can be positive role models—or your partner's father may have influenced them negatively. Either way, it helps to know in advance. Some individuals connect with their father-in-law more than their own. Or, perhaps your partner expects you to be a replica of their father.

44. What are five adjectives you would select to describe your relationship with your mother?

Are these words all negative, all positive, or a mixture? Mothers can be positive role models—or your partner's mother may have influenced them negatively. Either way, it helps to know in advance. Some individuals connect with their mother-in-law more than their own. Or, perhaps your partner expects you to be a replica of their mother.

45. These are all of the activities that I enjoy doing (list them). Of all these things, which ones wouldn't you enjoy doing with me?

Many couples discover that their partner never really enjoyed some of the activities they participated in with them prior to engagement. They participated just to be together. This ends up being courtship deception because it sends the message, "I like it now and will after marriage." Clear the air now. Each of you will probably have your own separate hobbies as well as those you do together. However, sharing nothing together does little for recreational intimacy.

46. What was the lowest point or most difficult time in your life, and how did you handle it?

It takes trust to share openly in this area. Treat what your partner says as a gift and handle it carefully. Sometimes sharing about this can answer other questions you have. We all carry some scars from the past, but if there's still an open wound, it may be best to wait for healing to happen.

47. Describe how you handle stress and frustration. What creates the greatest stress and frustration in your life?

You may have discovered the answer to this question already. Is your partner's response healthy and one you also would like to have, or does it frighten or concern you? Do they have a positive handle on dealing with this issue, or do they need more work? Is this a response you could live with for the rest of your life? If you have children, would you like them to observe this and follow the pattern?

48. How would you handle holidays, birthdays, special occasions, and so on, when it comes to your two families? What does gift giving mean in your family?

Now is the time to discuss traditions and expectations. What does your partner want to continue and discontinue? How flexible will your families be to changes you may want to make? What if gifts are very important to you and the other family doesn't give any? Or, what if they give lavish gifts and you have a set limit? Sometimes these issues need to be discussed with parents as well.

49. What is your dream or fantasy of a "perfect marriage"?

A person's fantasy can be shaped by what they've seen in real life, film, books, and so on. There is no perfect marriage because there are no perfect people. A marriage is an unconditional commitment of two imperfect people. It's better to talk about a *realistic* marriage. Why not interview several couples on the subject of what makes their marriage work and benefit from their experience?

50. What are three ways in which you see us as different? What are three ways in which you see us as similar? Which of these are you most comfortable with?

Couples are drawn together by differences as well as similarities. Sometimes we respond to differences because they fill our empty places. Sometimes we're comfortable with similarities. You may look at one another's differences now and say, "Oh, you're so *unique!*" After a couple years of marriage you may say, "I knew you were different—but not this much!" You may see their differences as wrong and set out on a crusade to make the other person into a revised edition of yourself.

Can you celebrate your differences now? If you can't now, you won't later! Consider this passage for your relationship: "Living as becomes you—with complete lowliness of mind (humility) and meekness (unselfishness, gentleness, mildness), with patience, bearing with one another *and* making allowances because you love one another" (Ephesians 4:2 AMP).

51. What qualities do you see in your parents that you expect to see in your future spouse?

Most of us have subtle unexpressed expectations that what is positive in our parents will stay with us forever because our spouse is likely to have the same traits or qualities. That can put a huge burden on your partner. Identify those qualities and evaluate your expectations. And speaking of parents, observe the way your partner treats their parent of the opposite sex. It's often a preview of what you can expect.

52. If I tell you I don't want to do something, or if I don't feel comfortable doing something you would like to do, how would you want to handle that?

Differences will arise. Each person may bring personal preferences to a relationship that are foreign to the other. Some may be all right, whereas others may not fit into a Christian framework. How does each of you handle a "no" from the other? It's time to find out.

53. Everyone brings some baggage into a relationship. What baggage are you bringing, and would it fit in an attaché case, a carry-on bag, a small suitcase, or a trunk?

We would all like to have our baggage fit in the attaché case, but nowadays there are expandable cases! Baggage could be rejections, abuse, promiscuity, homosexuality, substance abuse, financial problems, work or relationship instability, erratic faith practices, and so on. What's important is knowing there *is* baggage, identifying its effects and taking corrective steps to move forward in life.

54. How comfortable are you with confrontation or conflict? How do you usually resolve conflicts?

One of you may be accustomed to confrontation, and for the other, it's new. It may be second nature and a positive experience in your relationship, or a sign that it is in trouble. Perhaps you have wanted to discuss this but have been afraid to move in that direction. Talk about it. Where does anger enter into this issue? Anger expressed in a healthy, nonattacking way can build a relationship. Repressed or constantly held-in anger will eventually damage the person and the relationship.

55. When you marry, do you want children? If so, how many? Are you open to adoption? What training have you had to be a parent or stepparent?

Having children will change the relationship more than you realize. Your couple time together will be reduced by about 80 percent. Why do each of you want children, and why the number mentioned? If you differ on the numbers or on the adoption issue, work toward a resolution now. Please be open to taking classes and reading books together about parenting. Too often it is just the women who do this. It needs to be mutual.

56. What will your relationship be like with your parents, siblings, and friends after you marry? The same or different? If different, in what way?

Before taking the big step, spend time with your partner's family in all types of settings. Are the interactions you see loving and positive, or strained and obligatory? How do these compare with your experience? Their family members will be a part of your life, too. Time spent with each family will be diminished, but what gatherings will be a part of your life?

57. If you were to marry, what would be the hardest adjustment a person would have to make in order to live with you?

Don't expect an immediate answer to this question. Suggest that your partner reflect on it for a while. What they suggest could be a new revelation to you, or it could be something you expected.

58. How much do you value "personal time"—time to yourself to reflect, study, or recreate?

If your partner is an introvert—one who is drained by people and needs quiet, private time to recharge—and you're an extrovert, you'll need to work on understanding and accepting these differences, as well as not invading their private time. Or, you could be the introvert, and they need to be with people far more than you. Understanding how each other operates is key.

59. What is your idea of a "family"? What would you change about your family and how you were raised? What steps would you take to make these changes?

The more you know about your partner's family, the greater the insight you will have regarding their attitudes and beliefs about family. You'll discover why they have certain concerns, what their likes and dislikes are, and why they need from you what they do. We are shaped by our families but we may not want to re-create them. That's why you need a specific plan to follow to make those changes in your new family. Otherwise, you continue what you're used to and are comfortable with, even though you didn't like it.

60. What are your financial responsibilities and goals? How capable are you in budgeting, balancing checkbooks, shopping patterns? How stressful are these things to you? What debts do you have at this time, and have you ever filed for bankruptcy?

Finances are at the heart of so many conflicts in relationships. Each of you needs to know what one another earns as well as future potential. Have each of you used a budget? If not, begin working on it now if you proceed in your relationship. Is shopping a planned activity with financial resources in mind or is it a credit-card binge? Is shopping a delight or a chore? If a bankruptcy has occurred, it could affect future credit. Talk to a financial consultant about this. If this is a remarriage, what are the obligations to the former spouse and children? Would you want any of your resources going to them?

61. What has been the greatest amount of debt you've experienced?

This could have been a one-time debt, or it could be an ongoing accumulation that keeps building. What about college debt? Would you be expected to help with your partner's debt, and if so, what is your response to that? Do you have concerns about your partner pulling you into unwanted debt if you marry?

 P.S.

Remember this about money: God is the one who owns everything and you are a steward of His resources. He wants you to use it wisely and in such a way that it's a positive reflection upon Him.

62. How do you know you're in love with your partner?

Here are some healthy indications of love:

1. *Sharing Test.* Are you able to share together?

2. *Strength Test.* Does your love give you new strength and fill you with creative energy? Or does it take away your strength and energy?

3. *Respect Test.* Do you really have respect for each other?

4. *Habit Test.* Do you only *love* each other—or do you also *like* each other, and accept each other with your habits and shortcomings?

5. *Time Test.* Have you known each other long enough to know each other well?

6. *Separation Test.* Do you feel an unusual joy while in the company of each other? Is there pain in separation?

7. *Giving Test.* Are you in love to give? Are you capable of self-giving?

8. *Growth Test.* Is your love dynamic in its growth? Is it progressively maturing?

9. *Sex Test.* Is there mutual enjoyment of each other without the constant need of physical expression?

63. What do you think the Scripture means in Ephesians 5:25 and 22 when it says, "Husbands, love your wives just as Christ loved the church," and "Wives, submit yourselves to your husbands"?

An understanding of this biblical teaching is paramount. Too often, neither party has ever studied these passages in depth. Take the time to discuss them with knowledgeable individuals. These roles talk about each person's responsibility, not one's value. Remember, you have equal value before God.

64. If I could talk with your parents, what would they say I needed to know about you?

Does each of you really know how your parents see you now that you're an adult? It's true they may be biased in one way or another, but they have insights into lifelong patterns others may not see. Attempting to put yourself in their shoes may be insightful.

65. Who are you? (How would you describe who you are to another person?)

For many this is difficult. They may use personal characteristics and work ability, or they may express it from a spiritual dimension. We all need to know who we are and where we are going in life. How about you?

66. How would you complete these sentences?

❀ "In marriage, a wife should..."

❀ "In marriage, a husband should..."

"Shoulds" can be adjustable or set in stone. Adjustable expectations are part of the normal adjustment pattern of marriage and generate growth. Set-in-stone expectations create demands and strife. Sometimes they can be absolute expectations. It's best to discuss them now and clear the air. Not doing this before the wedding has disrupted many a honeymoon and hindered the growth of a marriage.

67. What are the experiences in life you would want the person you married to have had? What are the experiences in life you would *not* want the person you married to have had?

A strange question? Not really. You may think your partner is too sheltered or has been around too much. You might discover you're really different. How will this affect a lifelong relationship? Can you learn from one another? Do you believe your partner is damaged by these experiences or is naïve? Your response to what they say is critical. Your dreams and expectations may need to be adjusted accordingly.

68. Who are the couples that you know who have growing, healthy marriages?

If neither of you can think of any, please begin looking. If all you know are negative and dysfunctional couples, that could impact you. It's important to see how Jesus Christ can make a difference. These couples *do* exist!

69. On a scale of 0 to 10, to what extent do you experience guilt or anguish over your previous relationships? How might this guilt be affecting you in building a relationship with another individual?

Is this guilt or anguish realistic? What does it stem from? Has your partner discussed the relationship with someone who could help? To have a fulfilling relationship for the future, the ghosts of past relationships need to be put to rest. A new relationship is not a solution for guilt—experiencing God's forgiveness is.

70. What are the various jobs you've held, and for how long? What did you like and dislike about each one?

Commitment to work, as well as job stability, can be a pattern that affects relationships. Does your partner know what they want to do with their life, career-wise? Have they completed schooling, or is there more to come during marriage? How do you feel about their profession? Proud? Embarrassed? What do the likes and dislikes tell you?

71. What are your hobbies and interests aside from work? How much time and energy go into these, and would this change or stay the same if you were married? If you spend a lot of time on the computer or cell phone, how would you adjust this to work in a marriage?

Does your partner have any hobbies, or are they a workaholic? If they don't and you do, can they handle this? What do you have in common in this area? Is there something the two of you are open to exploring together? If your partner is very involved in some activities, do they expect to continue this involvement at the same level if they marry? Remember, you can't bring the single lifestyle into a marriage relationship.

72. If you were to marry, what would you receive from marriage that you wouldn't have if you were to remain single?

Don't just accept a few basic brief responses. Encourage your partner to think about this one for a while. There are many benefits to marriage, and it helps to identify them now. It may also reduce some of the fears that keep people from making commitments.

73. What has been your source of information about marriage? Parents, friends, classes, books? What would you do to learn more about marriage after you're married?

We all learn about marriage through the years. Is it accurate? Positive? Will it help or hinder the marital growth process? If your partner has never read a book on marriage, there are plenty of resources. Books and video series abound. So...it's time to get to work and expand your understanding of marriage.

74. What are the areas of your life you *must* control and those areas in your life you would like to control?

If your partner says, "I'm not in control of anything in my life," watch out. If your partner says, "I must be in control of everything in my life," watch out—that could include you. We all like to be in control in some areas, but few have thought this through. We're really not in control as much as we think we are. What's best is to learn to let God control our lives. And by the way, are you aware that the number-one reason for love dying after you're married is because of a controlling spouse? It's something to think about.

75. What television programs and movies have made an impact on your life and in what way?

Since movies and TV influence society and culture, they can also shape our personal beliefs, desires, and values. Listen to the program selection. It can speak volumes about who and what has impacted your partner. Are your tastes similar or dissimilar? Could you spend the rest of your life watching and listening to the same programs? If you were to marry, who would be in charge of the remote? Could you live without a TV? All of these are good to discuss before marriage.

76. During a conflict, a person either yields, withdraws, compromises, wins, or resolves. Which of these tends to be your style?

What causes conflicts? See James 4:1-3. There will be numerous conflicts throughout the life of a marriage. This isn't bad. It's normal. How you respond and deal with them is the real issue. How have they been resolved so far? It's actually an opportunity for growth in a relationship, but not if you always yield, withdraw, attempt to win, or even compromise. Work toward resolving the conflict so you both have your needs met and are satisfied with the resolution.

77. If you inherited a large sum of money and could afford to live anywhere in the world, where would it be? In addition, what would you love to do that you can't do now? How would you use the money? Would you still want me in your life?

Unlimited wealth can affect a person's values, lifestyle, beliefs, spiritual life, and who they spend the rest of their life with. Most people will never have this problem, but if it did happen, what would you do? This could be a new window into seeing who your partner really is and what is important to them. Being wealthy isn't the problem. It's how you let it affect your life. One positive is, the more you have, the more you can give to the Lord's work.

78. What was the best experience you've ever had at church, and what was the worst? How involved do you want to be in a local church?

Consider these questions for your own life as well. Often we let past experiences dictate our future. This can be positive or negative. If you're together in your level of involvement in church, it can draw you closer together.

79. What about your partner makes you proud of them?

Appreciation of your partner is important. It needs to be expressed—not just now, but regularly in the years ahead. It's a way of encouraging one another and lifting each other up in love. Some like to receive compliments in front of others, while others prefer it in privacy. Discover this now. If you're embarrassed in any way by what the other does, don't just keep it to yourself. Talk about this, too. Real love means you want the whole world to know who you're in love with and who they are!

80. If you could ask God any questions at this time, what would they be?

Perhaps neither of you have considered this question—but at some time in your life you will. Discussing it now may open the door to talking about it at any time. If a question is raised, don't attempt to answer it—just listen and reflect upon what your own questions would be.

81. Describe how you came to know the Lord. When was it? Who was involved? Where did it take place? How has your life changed?

For some, their conversion was dramatic, and for others it was very casual. For spiritual compatibility to develop, you need to know how each of you became a believer and where you are in this journey. It may take some time for your partner to reflect on this question.

82. What do you believe are five elements that make marriages work?

Perhaps your beliefs are similar, or they could be radically different. Once you identify them you can discuss how you would make sure these elements exist and continue to be enhanced. On the other hand, if there's no awareness of them, perhaps you need to investigate.

One fundamental element should be dedication, which, according to author and relationship expert Dr. Scott Stanley, is motivation based in a thoughtful decision to follow a certain path and give it your best.

83. In light of the number of divorces today, if you were to marry, why would your marriage last and not end up in divorce court?

Love is not enough, and being Christians doesn't guarantee success. You have to make your relationship a priority at all times. Marriage is a covenant—an unconditional commitment to an imperfect person—which means sticking to marriage and one another, rather than ending up stuck. If your partner (or you) doesn't have a game plan at this time, you need to get one!

84. What has been your experience with alcohol or drugs in the past and at the present time?

If there has been drug or alcohol use, what kind, to what extent, how recent was the usage, how did it stop, was there a treatment program, and what is your partner's intent for the future? You should also see if drug or alcohol use runs in the family.

85. How well do you handle constructive criticism and advice?

Take a moment and observe how your partner responds to this question. Do they welcome instruction and advice? Or, do they know everything already? Find out how they would like to be approached if you felt advice could be helpful. Also, ask who they are the most open to receiving advice from. If they answer "Anyone but you," watch out!

86. If marriage is on the horizon, are you planning to go through premarital counseling? After you're married, would you be open to seek marriage counseling if major concerns arise?

If a partner says, "I don't need any help—I know what I need to know," watch out! Everyone needs to be open to as much help as they can receive about marriage. If your partner doesn't want premarital counseling, what makes you think they would seek help after marriage?

87. What are the questions you have at this point in your life about sex? Do you wish you knew more when it comes to sex? Do you wish you knew less?

Our society is very open about sex and yet very ignorant. What we know about sex may not be healthy, and we may need some new information. If one partner is experienced and the other isn't, it could affect the adjustment process. Regardless of our backgrounds, it would be beneficial to read *Getting Your Sex Life off to a Great Start* by Cliff and Joyce Penner (W Publishing Group).

If one is willing to learn more and the other isn't, what does this tell you?

88. Of all the emotions we experience in life, what are the easiest ones for you to express and what are the most difficult?

Everyone is an emotional being. Some experience or express emotions more intensely than others. Some children are raised without an emotional or feeling vocabulary, so it is difficult for them as adults to express what they are experiencing inside. Talk about each of the following: fear, worry, anxiety, depression, sadness, anger, rage, frustration, guilt, shame, delight, sorrow, joy. (This will keep you busy for a while.)

89. What are the passions in life you would love doing, and which of those would be meaningful to you if I were to do them with you?

Togetherness in a relationship means being able to play, work, or serve together. Are each of you willing to at least try the other's passion? If nothing clicks, both of you could try something new in order to discover an interest you can do together. If there is nothing and you go ahead and marry, you could end up as a pair of married singles.

90. What foods do you enjoy, and what are your feelings about eating healthy?

Can food and diet really be a problem? Definitely, especially if one partner is weight-conscious or into the healthiest foods, and the other is a fast-food junkie on their way to breaking the high-cholesterol record. If you were to marry, how often would you eat in or go out? Who would have the final say on meals? And by the way, can either of you cook?

91. Politically, where do you find yourself—liberal, middle of the road, conservative, ultraconservative? Using the same scale, where do you find yourself spiritually?

Perhaps neither of you has ever labeled yourself politically before, but you need to think about it. Where does each of you stand on abortion and same-sex marriages? These issues are both political and spiritual. Do you both need to agree in this area, or can you allow differences? As you discuss, make sure that you both give ample support for your beliefs. Who has influenced these beliefs?

92. Do you feel you need to compromise or sacrifice anything to be a part of this relationship?

Relationships are based on give and take. They can't consist of all taking and no giving, or all giving and no taking. Balance is key. Make sure you learn what strikes a balance in the give-and-take arena for the both of you. Be wary if your partner feels their life is one giant compromise.

93. What are the five biggest fears in your life?

This can be a very revealing question. Couples can be married for years and never be aware their partner has any fears. How do these fears affect your relationship? How could you assist one another in overcoming these fears?

94. Do you like animals? What animal would you love to have as a pet that you don't or can't have at this time? How would you work it out if your partner wanted an animal and you didn't?

It's not just the animals that can be the issue—it's where they live and who takes care of them. What if one of you has allergies or fears about certain animals? If you married, what animals would be brought into the marriage?

95. If I messed up in a decision, whether in business or just in general, how would you share your frustration about my decision with me?

There's a big difference between "How could you have done that?" and "Tell me what happened." Attacking in anger won't help. Working toward a solution will. If your partner didn't tell you and you found out on your own, or if this turned out to be a constant problem, you probably will be upset. Make sure you keep the lines of communication open.

96. Who are the people in your life you've needed to forgive, and
how did you accomplish this?

Forgiveness is essential in any relationship. Have you seen forgiveness occur in your relationship, or is your partner a grudge
collector? Resentment will poison a relationship—even resent-
ments toward those other than you. Forgiveness is a process and
may take time. Both of you will need an abundance of this skill
if you marry. You'll learn it by experiencing God's forgiveness.

97. Take note of the fruits of the Spirit found in Galatians 5:22: "But the fruit of the Spirit is love, joy, peace, patience, kindness, goodness, faithfulness, gentleness, and self-control. Against such things there is no law." On a scale of 0-10, where do you see yourself on each one of the traits at this point in your life?

A relationship built upon the teaching of God's Word has the best foundation for a fulfilled marriage. Do you look to the Scriptures as the basis for the way to respond to one another? If not, it's not too late to begin.

98. How frequently do you have contact with your former partner, if any, and in what way? What is the purpose of the contact? What feelings do you experience on these occasions?

Some believe they can "just be friends" with a former partner. But why? Is the relationship really over? Why spend time with someone when there is no future? And if your partner is really interested in you, it would seem the time and energy would be directed to you. If your partner says they have no feelings, ask again. It's rare to be neutral.

99. Do you believe you and I should be honest about everything in our relationship, or should some things be kept private? If I asked your past partners if you were honest and trustworthy, how would they answer?

Sometimes people let things slide during courtship in order to not rock the boat. They may even think they'll sway you after you're married. It won't work. You need a person who is truthful and doesn't bend the truth in any way. You need a partner who is honest with themselves and doesn't practice self-deception. You need a person who is honest with you.

100. How many times have you been married (including any annul-
ments)?

Sometimes a partner may *forget* to tell you about a brief marriage or annulment. If so, what else aren't they telling you?
Sometimes people say, "Well, the first one really didn't count
because we were so young, and it only lasted six months." A
marriage is a marriage. If they were formally married, did they
attend a divorce recovery group? It's necessary. How long ago
was the divorce? It usually takes two to three years to recover.
(See "If You've Been Married Before..." at the back of this book
for more to think about.)

101. What do you envision in the future for this relationship?

After answering this question and the preceding ones, are you confident there is a healthy future for both of you? Are there some areas that need further discussion? Take the time to go over these problem areas and pray about them. Make sure you take time to celebrate all that you do have in common. You should now have a good foundation for building a life together. If you discover that you're not as compatible as you first thought, or if too many red flags were raised during your discussions, it's best to know that now and back out of the relationship rather than end up in an unhealthy marriage to a stranger.

Three

*I*f You've Been
Married Before

I. Describe your expectations for your new marriage:

II. What was the situation like with your former marriage? Let's compare it to the situation with your new prospective partner.

    1. a. How long did you know your previous spouse before you began to date?

    b. How long did you know your current partner before you began to date?

    2. a. What attracted you to your former spouse?

    b. What attracted you to your current partner?

3. a. How long did you date your former spouse before deciding to marry?

b. How long did you date your prospective spouse before deciding to think seriously about engagement?

4. a. What were your reasons for wanting to marry your former partner?

    1)

    2)

    3)

    4)

    5)

b. What are your reasons for considering marriage to your current partner?

1)

2)

3)

4)

5)

5. What dreams did you have for your prior marriage?

6. What dreams do you have for your prospective marriage?

III. How would you describe your former and present partners?

    1. List ten adjectives that describe your former spouse.

      1)   6)

      2)   7)

      3)   8)

      4)   9)

      5)   10)

    2. List ten adjectives that describe your prospective spouse.

      1)   6)

      2)   7)

      3)   8)

      4)   9)

      5)   10)

Now indicate with a check mark the adjectives in both lists that describe you.

3. <u>Underline</u> any of the following descriptions that apply to you. Place a check mark (✓) by any that apply to your former spouse. (Circle) any that apply to your prospective spouse.

Perfectionistic tendencies	Overworks	Sleeps too much
Compulsive behavior	Procrastination	Difficulty at work
Type A behavior	Smokes	Insomnia
Risk-taker	Suicidal threats	Crying
Impulsive behavior	Suicidal behavior	Use of pornography
Loss of control	Withdraws from others	Aggressive behavior
Use of drugs	Worry	Verbally abusive
Use of alcohol	Depression	Physically abusive
Overeats	Low self-esteem	Lazy

4. Describe the pattern of marital satisfaction in your previous marriage, filling in the appropriate months or years on the timeline below.

First year   End of Marriage

a. Indicate on the chart when the conflicts started, what they were about, and how they manifested themselves.

b. What did you do to improve the relationship?

c. Indicate on the chart when the decision to divorce was made, and who decided.

d. How long did the divorce process take?

e. Describe in detail how your divorce has impacted and changed you.

f. What will you bring into your prospective marriage from the previous marriage?

g. What do you *not* want to bring into your next marriage, and how will you avoid this?

5. Describe the pattern of marital satisfaction you predict you will have in your prospective marriage:

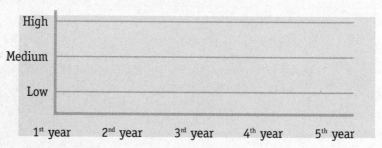

Now describe specifically what you will do to make this a reality:

6. In what way is your present relationship similar to your former one?

7. In what way is your present relationship different from your former one?

IV. Now compare the expectations you listed at the beginning of this questionnaire with these realistic expectations of any second marriage.[8]

1. You can expect it to be tougher than a first marriage.

2. You can expect it to be complicated, exasperating, and tiring.

3. You can expect it to be a slow building process.

4. You can expect some "same old script" at times—but know that you are writing a new script each day.

5. You can expect to want to run from it every now and then—but you won't.

6. You can expect a lot of outside pressures that are new to you. They come from parents, children, families, jobs, and former spouses.

7. You can expect your second marriage to be successful if you can dig in and go for the long haul, instead of the overnight wonder.

8. You can expect frequent visits from ghosts of your previous marriage, but a good blast of reality will make them disappear.

9. You can expect *not* to become a "second-marriage failure" statistic.

10. You can expect not to run when the going gets tough, nor do you intend to serve a sentence called "marriage." You can expect to solve the problems that cause the "run or rust" mentality in a second marriage.

11. You can expect this marriage to be different because you have learned many things from the failure of your first marriage.

12. You can expect this marriage to become a "working model" for all to watch and encourage.

*L*ist of Recommended Reading for Couples

Boundaries in Dating by Dr. Henry Cloud and Dr. John Townsend (Zondervan, 2000)

Should We Stay Together? by Jeffrey Larson (John Wiley & Sons, 2000)

How Can I Be Sure? by Bob Phillips (Harvest House, 1999)

The Purpose-Drive Life by Rick Warren (Zondervan, 2002)

Before You Say "I Do"™ *Devotional* by H. Norman Wright (Harvest House, 2003)

Communication: Key to Your Marriage by H. Norman Wright (Regal Books, 2000)

Starting Out Together by H. Norman Wright (Regal Books, 1996)

Notes

1. Barbara De Angelis, Ph.D., *Are You the One For Me?* (New York: Delacorte Press, 1992), pp. 91-100.
2. Jeffrey Larson, Ph.D., *Should We Stay Together?* (San Francisco, CA: John Wiley & Sons, Inc., 2000), p. 118.
3. H. Norman Wright, *Relationships That Work: and Those That Don't* (Ventura, CA: Regal Books, 1998), pp. 116-18.
4. Rachel Safiew with Wendy Roberts, *There Goes the Bride* (San Francisco, CA: John Wiley & Sons, Inc., 2003), pp. 5-10, 119.
5. Adapted from Larson, pp. 165-66.
6. Dr. Paul Tournier, *The Healing of Persons* (New York: Harper Collins, 1965), p. 88.
7. Dr. Dwight Small, *After You've Said I Do* (Westwood, N.J.: Fleming H. Revell, 1968), p. 75.
8. Jim Smoke, *Growing Through Remarriage* (Grand Rapids, MI: Fleming H. Revell, 1990), pp. 90-91

Other Harvest House Books
by H. Norman Wright

❀ ❀ ❀

Quiet Times for Couples

Designed to stimulate genuinely open communication between husband and wife, each day's devotion makes it easy for couples to share about the deeper parts of their lives.

Before You Say "I Do"®

Couples will explore how to clarify role expectations, establish a healthy sexual relationship, handle finances, and acquire a solid understanding of how to develop a biblical relationship.

Before You Remarry

Couples will discover how to make their future marriages successful by covering remarriage basics and communication skills; establishing realistic expectations; and handling problems, including in-laws, merged families, and sexual issues.

After You Say "I Do" Devotional

Celebrating marriage, encouraging open communication, and providing keys to greater intimacy, these devotions offer readers a wealth of practical ideas and suggestions that will bring more joy into their unions and enrich their relationship.

Finding the Right One for You

A must for every person seeking God's direction and wise counsel, this straight-talking book is rich with guidelines and practical exercises developed by marriage enrichment expert Norm Wright. Designed to help people in the process of dating make choices that will lead to the kind of marriage they've always longed for.

Other Good
Harvest House Reading

MEN ARE LIKE WAFFLES—WOMEN ARE LIKE SPAGHETTI
by *Bill and Pam Farrel*

Men keep life elements in separate boxes; women intertwine everything. Providing biblical insights, sound research, and humorous anecdotes, the Farrels explore gender differences and preferences and how they can strengthen relationships.

101 WAYS TO GET AND KEEP HIS ATTENTION
by *Michelle McKinney Hammond*

From her survey of more than a hundred eligible men, noted relationship author Michelle McKinney Hammond paints a realistic picture of what really attracts men to women and what to do with his attention once you've got it.

THE HUSBAND PROJECT
by *Kathi Lipp*

Through simple daily action plans, Kathi Lipp shows wives how they can bring the fun back into their relationship even amidst their busy schedules. This book is for every woman who desires to bring more joy into her marriage but just needs a little help setting a plan into action.

HARVEST HOUSE PUBLISHERS
EUGENE, OREGON